PROMISES FROM GOD FOR
PARENTS

PROMISES FROM GOD FOR
PARENTS

T. D. JAKES

BERKLEY PRAISE, NEW YORK

THE BERKLEY PUBLISHING GROUP
Published by the Penguin Group
Penguin Group (USA) Inc.
375 Hudson Street, New York, New York 10014, USA
Penguin Group (Canada), 90 Eglinton Avenue East, Suite 700, Toronto, Ontario M4P 2Y3, Canada
(a division of Pearson Penguin Canada Inc.)
Penguin Books Ltd., 80 Strand, London WC2R 0RL, England
Penguin Group Ireland, 25 St. Stephen's Green, Dublin 2, Ireland (a division of Penguin Books Ltd.)
Penguin Group (Australia), 250 Camberwell Road, Camberwell, Victoria 3124, Australia
(a division of Pearson Australia Group Pty. Ltd.)
Penguin Books India Pvt. Ltd., 11 Community Centre, Panchsheel Park, New Delhi—110 017, India
Penguin Group (NZ), Cnr. Airborne and Rosedale Roads, Albany, Auckland 1310, New Zealand
(a division of Pearson New Zealand Ltd.)
Penguin Books (South Africa) (Pty.) Ltd., 24 Sturdee Avenue, Rosebank, Johannesburg 2196,
South Africa

Penguin Books Ltd., Registered Offices: 80 Strand, London WC2R 0RL, England

PROMISES FROM GOD FOR PARENTS

This book is an original publication of The Berkley Publishing Group.

Copyright © 2006 by Bishop T. D. Jakes.
Text design by Tiffany Estreicher.

Unless otherwise noted, Scripture quotations are from the *Holy Bible*, Contemporary English Version,
copyright © 1995 by American Bible Society, New York, New York. Used by permission. Scripture
quotations identified as * are from the *Holy Bible*, New Living Translation, copyright © 1996. Used by
permission of Tyndale House Publishers, Inc., Wheaton, Illinois 60189. All rights reserved. Scripture
quotations noted as † are from the *Holy Bible*, New International Version. Copyright © 1973, 1978,
1984 International Bible Society. Used by permission of Zondervan Bible Publishers.

FIRST EDITION: August 2006

Library of Congress Cataloging-in-Publication Data

Jakes, T. D.
 Promises from God for parents / T. D. Jakes. — 1st ed.
  p. cm.
  ISBN 0-425-21001-4
  1. Parents—Religious life. 2. God—Promises. I. Title.

 BV4529.J35 2006
 242'.645—dc22

2006013199

PRINTED IN THE UNITED STATES OF AMERICA

10 9 8 7 6 5 4 3 2 1

I would like to dedicate this book to Jamar, Jermaine, Cora, Sarah, and Dexter. Thanks for all the things that your mother and I have learned about life and love from being your parents. Loving you through good times and bad times has given us the slightest inkling of God's love and patience with us. It is through praying for you that we have learned God's promises to parents.

ACKNOWLEDGMENTS

My gratitude to my wife, Serita, and my entire family, who generously shared me with this manuscript. Thank you for being such a blessed gift in my life everyday. I also want to acknowledge the compassion and encouragement that I consistently receive from my church family.

Thank you, Denise Silvestro, for your insights and creativity, and for working tirelessly to bring my message to fruition.

Thank you Joel Fotinos, for your enthusiasm, encouragement, wisdom, and for continuing to believe in me.

Thank you to everyone at Penguin. You always treat me and my work with great dignity and integrity. My gratitude to Susan Petersen Kennedy, Leslie Gelbman, Ivan Held, Marilyn Ducksworth, Craig Burke, Heather Connor, Norman Lidofsky, Patrick Nolan, Chris Mosley, Katie Day, Lara Robbins, and everyone at the Noble Group.

CONTENTS

INTRODUCTION

I t wasn't very long ago that a young couple at the church celebrated the birth of their first child. I remember the look of pride on the new father's face as people were congratulating him over the good news announcement. His smile was so wide and his eyes sparkled so bright that you would have thought he was the first man ever to father a child. His joy was a beautiful sight to behold.

About three months later I saw him again at church. The change that had come upon him was dramatic, to say the least. His eyes, which once shined brightly, now had a dull, bloodshot look to them, and bags under them. His smile was nowhere to be found. His shoulders slumped as he tiredly went through the motions of worship. It was obvious that the joy he had felt had turned into heaviness.

What made the difference? Before the child was born, the

father had had visions and ideas of how parenting would be. It was an idyllic dream, one that had made him happy. He had believed that his child would be smart and sweet, would never cry, and would sleep like, well, a baby. But any parent of a newborn can verify that the reality is quite different from the dream. Sleepless nights, bone-aching exhaustion, and the fear that you can't do anything right, replace the fantasy that most of us have before we are parents. Not to mention the obvious: Children do not come with instruction manuals. Parents are left to figure out how to raise a child as they go along.

Now, I'd be the first to tell you that being a parent is a mighty blessing. There are plenty of times for hugs, kisses, and sweet and tender moments. But in the case of parenting children, the cliché is actually true: Anything worthwhile requires a lot of hard work.

I wanted to write this book for parents with children of all ages because parenting can sometimes be hard work. Through all phases and stages—from the newborn to the college-bound and beyond—children can confuse us, fatigue us, and frustrate us. Yes, they can bring us great joy, and, yes, they can be our greatest blessing. But that is only true if you are able to see through the pain that comes with the journey of parenting to the larger picture: God has chosen you to be a parent for a reason.

Prepare the Feast

As a Christian parent, you have help in the Bible, your church community, and most importantly, your Heavenly

Father. He is always available for guidance, for strength, and for patience. And trust me, you'll need some patience! He can provide all that you need to successfully manage the rules, the regulations, and the responsibilities of being a parent. You don't have to do it alone.

Jesus tells us the story of the parent who loved his children so much, that when one of them left home, acting irresponsible and squandering his money, until he had no choice but to return to his father's house, instead of condemning the boy and banning him, the father welcomed the son with open arms. It is the parable of the Prodigal Son, and is one of the most widely quoted parables in the Bible. But have you ever wondered what Jesus was really getting at in this story beyond the obvious lesson? I believe that one of the keys of this tale is found when the father welcomes back the son and tells his servants to prepare a feast. Here was a boy who had left his home and squandered his father's fortune and was now back with empty pockets and an empty spirit. There was no "I told you so," no condemnation, and no attempts to make the child feel guilt and shame. No. Instead, that father saw his son in the distance and rushed out to him, embracing him in the way only a parent can.

And then he called for the feast:

> But his father said to the servants, "Hurry and bring the best clothes and put them on him. Give him a ring for his finger and sandals for his feet. Get the best calf and prepare it, so we can eat and celebrate. This son of mine was dead, but has now come back to life. He was lost and has now been found." And they began to celebrate.
>
> (LUKE 15:22–24)

The father did not withhold anything from his child. As Christian parents, we are called to be Christlike in our parenting. That doesn't mean that you should not issue consequences for improper behavior, for that will help to shape and mold a child to be prepared to live in the world. What it does mean is that you should never, ever, ever withhold your love from your children. Rush to your child. Always be the first to bring a solution to any problem. Pray for guidance and the ability to be larger than any grievance or situation that occurs.

Now, you might be saying to yourself right about now, "That sounds good, but my child disrespected me, and I will not tolerate disrespect." I say to you, there is a difference between teaching a child to respect you, and teaching a child to fear you. As the Prodigal Son parable shows, your duty as a Christian parent is to be the example, not the problem. If that sounds too difficult, take comfort in knowing that God has not and will never give you anything that is too difficult for you to bear. Take a moment to think about how your Father treats you. Turn it around. In this story, you are the child, and God is the Father who rushes toward you. His promise to you is that He always will. Your promise to your children is that you always will rush to them.

There are parents who have lost a child. It's the most tragic loss I can imagine. I believe if you could sit down with parents who have lost a child, they would tell you what they tell me, which is that they would give anything to have even ten minutes more with their child. Let us learn from those tragedies, and cherish our children while we can.

Promises from God

Parenting is a huge responsibility, and truthfully, that is the point. It is not meant to be easy. These promises are here to remind you of the great responsibility, as well as the great joy, found in parenting. But in the midst of the great responsibility, God always is asking you to let Him help. Every promise in the Bible is really one promise, which is that God will never forsake you. If you can learn that one truth, you can face any challenge and reap every reward. You have to have faith, and I know you want to have faith or you wouldn't have picked up this book. Take that faith, and multiply it, invest in it, and watch it grow.

God never breaks His promises. Never. He will answer those who seek Him. You have to do your part. Your part is to keep faith. Just because it seems difficult doesn't mean God is not there by your side. Just because a situation seems impossible doesn't mean He won't help you overcome it. All things are possible through God, and He will make all things possible for you.

Throughout these pages you will find some of God's promises for you. When you are troubled, look to His Word and be heartened. When you are in darkness, find comfort in His Life. I have chosen twelve topics I have seen touch parents the most, but if you don't see a specific subject that you are looking for, just dive in—God's Word covers everything.

At the end of this book, you will find Promise Pages. It is here that you should remind yourself of the promises that God has made you and the promises He has fulfilled. Remember that God is the Promise Keeper.

God promises you so much. Don't you think you should make promises to Him in return? The Promise Pages are where you can record *your* promises to the Lord. Exchange vows with God your Father. He will be by your side in good times and in bad, through every stage and every age of parenting. You are never alone. Wherever you are, God is with you.

LOVE

LOVE

Love is kind and patient,
never jealous, boastful,
*   proud, or rude.*
Love isn't selfish
*   or quick tempered.*
It doesn't keep a record
*   of wrongs that others do.*
*   (1 Corinthians 13:4–5)*

A parent's love for a child is a mighty force. And yet, it sometimes seems that our children can test us like no others. At times they seem ungrateful, disrespectful, selfish, and downright defiant. Just ask any parent who lives with a teenager! But although we may be pushed so far as to lose our temper, we should always remember that our children are precious gifts from God. A child is a living, breathing testament that our Father loves us and is honoring us by entrusting us with the care of one of His children. What a responsibility! We get to be God's earthly counterpart, caring for our children the way that He cares for us. Love your children the way God loves you—faithfully and unconditionally.

Your Promise to God . . .

Sometimes that child just wears on my last nerve! But, Heavenly Father, I will use Your example and embrace him with a fierce, steadfast love.

LOVE

"Cut the baby in half ! That way each of you can have part of him."

"Please don't kill my son," the baby's mother screamed. "Your Majesty, I love him very much, but give him to her. Just don't kill him."

The other woman shouted, "Go ahead and cut him in half. Then neither of us will have the baby."

Solomon said, "Don't kill the baby." Then he pointed to the first woman, "She is his real mother. Give the baby to her."

(1 Kings 3:25–27)

I've seen the fire in my wife's eyes when someone attempts to do something she even thinks might hurt her babies. Let me tell you, I'd get out of the way and run for cover if I were that person! A mother forms a bond with her child even before it is born. She provides nourishment, oxygen, safety, and warmth to the precious life within her womb. And even though the umbilical cord is cut when the child enters this world, the bond between mother and child is never severed. She'll protect that child with her life and make sacrifices for the benefit or her baby. Well, let me speak for children everywhere when I say, "Mamas, thank you for always looking out for your babies!"

YOUR PROMISE TO GOD . . .

Thank You, Lord, for the precious gift You bestowed upon me when You made me a parent. I vow to protect Your children whom You have entrusted to me.

LOVE

The Lord is merciful!
He is kind and patient,
    and his love never fails.
The Lord won't always be angry
    and point out our sins;
        (Psalm 103:8–9)

No matter what you do or say, that child of yours always seems to be getting into trouble. If it isn't one thing, it's another. You just don't know what else you can do.

I'll tell you what to do: Show your child love no matter what. Yes, sometimes love means expressing anger and disappointment, imposing a punishment and setting limits. But as our Heavenly Father forgives us and shows us unconditional love, so should we always love our children, so that we may lift them up and help them become better people.

YOUR PROMISE TO GOD . . .

Jesus, through You, our sins were forgiven. Your Father's mercy and Your blood washed us clean and restored us. When my child misbehaves, I will remember Your example and show him love and patience.

LOVE

My child, don't turn away
or become bitter
  when the Lord corrects you.
The Lord corrects
  everyone he loves,
just as parents correct
  their favorite child.
    (Proverbs 3:11–12)

The mother who never punishes her child is not more loving. The father who never sets limits may seem like his son's friend, but actually does more harm than good. Children need boundaries. They need correction when they have done wrong. It is the loving parent who puts her child back on the right track when he has misstepped.

Similarly, when we deviate from the path of holiness, our Father lovingly corrects us and sets us back in the right direction. At times, this correction is uncomfortable and unwelcomed, but although it may be difficult, know that it is God showing that He loves you.

YOUR PROMISE TO GOD . . .

Like a parent who knows what is best for her child, You, Lord, know what's best for me. I will walk the path You lay before me even when it seems like a rocky road.

LOVE

I have loved you even as the Father has loved me.
Remain in my love.

(John 15:9*)

When Jesus asks you to remain in His love, He is asking you to be faithful to His love and obey Him completely. Not some of the time, not only on those things you like or that are easy, but in all areas. Sometimes this is hard to do. Sometimes you may be tempted to put your needs and the needs of your family before His commandments to you. But don't you realize God knows what you need better than you do? He only wants the best for His children and won't let you settle for anything less. If you follow Him, He will reveal His plans and visions for your life—and His vision is more glorious than anything you could have imagined for yourself.

YOUR PROMISE TO GOD . . .

I will remain in Your love and obey You completely.

LOVE

The people of Zion said,
"The Lord has turned away
  and forgotten us."

The Lord answered,
"Could a mother forget a child
  who nurses at her breast?
Could she fail to love an infant
  who came from her own body?
Even if a mother could forget,
  I will never forget you."
        (Isaiah 49:14–15)

Your son is in trouble at school again. Your daughter is running around with that boy who is nothing but bad news. And on top of all this, your baby is sick . . . again. Sometimes it seems so overwhelming. You try to be a good parent. You try hold your family together, but sometimes the weight upon your shoulders is just too heavy and the road is too steep.

Relax. The Lord is always there to carry your burden and bring you relief. Offer up to Him your troubles and He will lighten your load. He will not forsake you. He is always there to lend you a hand.

Your Promise to God . . .

When times are tough and I feel overwhelmed, I will look to You to bring me peace.

DISCIPLINE

DISCIPLINE

"Blessed is the man whom God corrects;
so do not despise the discipline of the
    Almighty."

          (Job 5:17[†])

Sometimes just the word "discipline" can make someone break out in a cold sweat. It feels hard and mean and like you are in trouble. Discipline, however, is a tool that God uses to bring about positive change in the heart and actions of every person. See discipline for what it is: a way of helping your children become the best they can be. Use it positively, and with the right motivation, and it will yield amazing results.

YOUR PROMISE TO GOD . . .

I will follow Your example and lovingly correct my children.

DISCIPLINE

Invest in truth and wisdom,
discipline and good sense,
    and don't part with them.
        (Proverbs 23:23)

When we think of parenting and discipline, we usually think of how the parent will punish the child who does something wrong. But I'd like you to think about it this way: Discipline is a way to sharpen and deepen your children's understanding of how to live a righteous life. By correcting your children, you will have to correct them less often. Discipline of the mind will decrease discipline of their actions. (It works for the parents as well!)

YOUR PROMISE TO GOD . . .

I will correct my children as needed and teach them to live as children of God.

DISCIPLINE

"The Lord corrects people
he loves
and disciplines those
he calls his own."
(Hebrews 12:6)

Did you ever stop to realize that Jesus' disciples became so only after they developed discipline? Discipline was a necessary part of their learning before they could follow the Lord with open hearts. Being a good parent requires you to help your children learn the lessons of discipline so that they may realize their great potential—for God has great plans for them . . . and for you!.

YOUR PROMISE TO GOD . . .

I will teach my children the way of the Lord and help them stay on the path of righteousness.

DISCIPLINE

If you correct your children,
they will bring you peace
and happiness.
(Proverbs 29:17)

We've all been in a public place where a child begins to wail and scream and misbehave, and the parents seem to do nothing. Doing nothing actually increases the child's poor behavior, whereas strong and firm discipline will create guidelines that your child can live within. When he misbehaves, he will know that there are consequences. Don't forget that the reverse is also true. When your child behaves well, in public or at home, reward her with positive feedback, a hug, or some special time together. Rewards, used properly, can be a way of tangibly letting your children know when they do well. Give them something to work toward, rather than something to work against.

YOUR PROMISE TO GOD . . .

I will respond appropriately to my child's behavior—good and bad—punishing actions that need correcting, but rewarding those that deserve praise.

DISCIPLINE

No discipline is enjoyable while it is happening—it is painful! But afterward there will be a quiet harvest of right living for those who are trained in this way.

(Hebrews 12:11*)

All parents know that there are times when it seems like their children are in a constant state of misbehaving. They test you constantly; they talk back and throw things; they ignore your warnings. It almost seems as if they are daring you to discipline them. They are. Even though their actions and words may be saying one thing, do not forget that, deep down, they are saying something else. They are saying, "Please help me. Please give me rules so I know how to behave. Please correct me to show me you care."

Your Promise to God . . .

As You correct me to show that You love me, I will correct my children so that they will know that they are loved.

DISCIPLINE

So keep in mind that the Lord has been correcting you, just as parents correct their children.

(Deuteronomy 8:5)

Parents sometimes get the wrong impression, thinking they are to "correct" their children because they are older and wiser. And while that is true to a certain point, the greater truth is that parents must never forget that they, too, are being corrected by God. Our Father keeps a close eye on each and every parent, gently guiding and leading them. As the parent learns and grows, so do the children. Always correct your children with the humbleness of one who is being corrected by God.

YOUR PROMISE TO GOD . . .

I will listen for Your correction, knowing that You are leading me to greater things.

DESPAIR

DESPAIR

I've commanded you to be strong and brave. Don't ever be afraid or discouraged! I am the Lord your God, and I will be there to help you wherever you go.

(Joshua 1:9)

Kids love to read comic books about superheroes—the Man of Steel, Wonder Woman, and other characters with superhuman powers. But they have some of the greatest heroes living under their very own roofs. Mothers and fathers everywhere face daily challenges, big and small, trying to keep their households together. I know. I, too, am a parent, and have faced crying babies, sick toddlers, and troubled teens, not to mention financial responsibilities, a challenging job, and demands on my time, energy, and resources. Sometimes it seems overwhelming.

What parents have to realize is that they have a superhero looking out for them, too. Our Heavenly Father stands by us and gives us strength, courage, and the ability to conquer all the challenges we face. With Him by our side, nothing is insurmountable.

Your Promise to God . . .

When things get tough, I will remember that I have You, the mightiest of heroes, to help me through.

DESPAIR

When his people pray for help,
he listens and rescues them
*   from their troubles.*
The Lord is there to rescue
all who are discouraged
*   and have given up hope.*
*   (Psalm 34:17–18)*

In times of darkness, there is always light—if you seek it. Simply pray to God and He will be there to lift you out of the shadows and into the brightness of His eternal love. Pray, sing a hymn, spend some quiet time, or just talk to the Lord. All you have to do is reach out to Him. No matter what you face, our Lord is there to assist you. There is no trouble big enough that He cannot overcome. Just call on Him and He will rescue you from despair.

YOUR PROMISE TO GOD . . .

In my darkness I will look to You, and You will be my light.

DESPAIR

If you obey the laws and teachings that the Lord gave Moses, you will be successful. Be strong and brave and don't get discouraged or be afraid of anything.

(1 Chronicles 22:13)

There's so much to do and no one to help you do it. As a parent, you must fill many roles: mentor, disciplinarian, breadwinner, cook, housekeeper, chauffeur, and tutor. And that's just the start of if. Husband/wife, employee, friend, and possibly your parents' caretaker, are other hats that you may wear. You're overwhelmed and frustrated by all you have to do and you just don't know where to turn for help. Well, I'll tell you where to turn. There is something that can bolster you and will never let you down. Turn to the Word and let the holy teachings give you strength. Trust Scripture and read it daily. It will give you the support you need.

YOUR PROMISE TO GOD . . .

I will read Your Word daily. It will be my guide and my support.

DESPAIR

But now you feel discouraged
when struck by trouble.
You respect God and live right,
so don't lose hope!

(Job 4:5–6)

Crises strike every family some time or another. Death, illness, financial strain, betrayal, disappointment, or relationship woes—trouble will knock on your door eventually to pay a visit to your house. Don't despair! When you keep God at the center of your home, there is nothing that can topple it. Let your faith fortify your family, protecting it from soul-draining hopelessness. Know that as children of God you are always protected.

YOUR PROMISE TO GOD . . .

I will keep You front and center in my home, for You will keep us safe.

DESPAIR

Why am I discouraged?
Why am I restless?
  I trust you!
And I will praise you again
because you help me,
  and you are my God.
  (Psalm 42:11)

Trusting in God means letting go of all your worries and handing them over to the Lord. He will free you from the grip of despair and comfort you in His safe embrace. Don't you know that all your worry won't do a lick of good? Don't waste the energy. Instead, focus exclusively on the goodness of the Lord and know that He will take care of you. Sing His praises and take solace in the fact that He is your Father, walking every step of the way with you.

YOUR PROMISE TO GOD . . .

I will sing a song of praise and celebrate Your glory.

DESPAIR

Praise God, the Father of our Lord Jesus Christ! The Father is a merciful God, who always gives us comfort. He comforts us when we are in trouble, so that we can share that same comfort with others in trouble.

(2 Corinthians 1:3–4)

The other mothers in the PTA wonder how you do it. The fellow fathers at the Little League game want to know your secret. The brothers and sisters at church admire your fortitude and always turn to you for help. No, you're not perfect. You, too, have your share of obstacles to overcome. So how do you manage to stay steady in the face of all that challenges you?

It is by being firmly rooted in your faith that you are able to withstand the winds of trouble when they blow across your life. It's no secret. Shout it from the rooftop. Spread the Good Word. Jesus is our Savior and He is the source of our peace.

YOUR PROMISE TO GOD . . .

You are the source of peace. I praise You, Lord Jesus Christ.

PATIENCE

PATIENCE

Patience and gentle talk
can convince a ruler
and overcome any problem.
(Proverbs 25:15)

In the grocery store checkout line, I observed a young mother and her toddler in front of me. I braced for the inevitable. You see, store owners cleverly keep racks of candy by the counters, knowing that people can be tempted to make such impulse buys. The patrons most tempted by such displays are young children. Once they spot the candy, they ask, beg, scream, cry, cajole, and even throw full-blown tantrums—all for a taste of the sweets.

As I waited in line, I expected the young boy in front of me to start demanding some candy. Well, he asked. He even pleaded in that whiny voice only a child can master. But that's as far as it went. His mother bent down, smiled, and promised he could pick out a candy bar they would buy the *next time*, if he was good today. She didn't scold him or even give him a stern look. Her simple, patient words reined him in and quieted him down. The sweetness in her tone was sweets enough for the young child that day.

Your Promise to God . . .

When my child gets demanding, I will hold my temper and use words of kindness.

PATIENCE

For examples of patience in suffering, dear brothers and sisters, look at the prophets who spoke in the name of the Lord. We give great honor to those who endure under suffering. Job is an example of a man who endured patiently. From his experience we see how the Lord's plan finally ended in good, for he is full of tenderness and mercy.

(James 5:10–11*)

Any parent who has spent countless sleepless nights tending to a newborn who has her days and nights mixed up knows. Any parent who has struggled through the "terrible twos," which seems to spill over into the threes and fours, knows. Any parent who has dealt with the physical and mental exhaustion that comes from caring for a sick child or helping the child navigate the rough waters of adolesence or worrying about a teenager with a driver's license knows. They all know that, even without the extraordinarily difficult circumstances that some families face, being a parent is tough work.

As you struggle through the normal phases and stages of parenting, be patient and persevere. Your reward will come in the heart-melting smile of your baby, tiny arms wrapped tightly around your neck in a hug, and the satisfaction of seeing your child grow into a successful, God-loving adult.

YOUR PROMISE TO GOD . . .

Through the sleepless nights, worry, and exhaustion, I will remain patient knowing that God will reward me for my efforts.

PATIENCE

Be patient and trust the Lord.
Don't let it bother you
when all goes well for those
who do sinful things.
(Psalm 37:7)

Look at them! They live in a big house, drive the newest cars, are prospering financially, and seem to have the perfect children. Your neighbors seem quite blessed, but you know their morals are questionable, their means to success tainted by impropriety. Why do things go well for them, while you, faithful servant of God, struggle to get by?

Stop being bothered by their good fortune—that is not your business. They will be judged accordingly by Someone far greater than you. Instead, keep your eyes focused on the Lord, for in His own time He will bring you great reward.

YOUR PROMISE TO GOD . . .

I will wait patiently for You and trust that You are looking out for me.

PATIENCE

Never give up. Eagerly follow the Holy Spirit and serve the Lord. Let your hope make you glad. Be patient in time of trouble and never stop praying.

(Romans 12:11–12)

Whatever crisis you face, pray through it. Whatever obstacle you must overcome, pray on it. Whatever miracle you are desperate for, pray for it. In times of trouble, when all seems lost, walk toward the Lord. If you can't walk, crawl. If you're too weak to crawl just reach out to Him. He will be there. He will save you. He will never forsake you.

YOUR PROMISE TO GOD . . .

Lord, in good times and bad, I will serve You faithfully, and I know that You will always be there for me.

PATIENCE

Learn to be patient, so that you will please God and be given what he has promised.

(Hebrews 10:36)

The kids are fighting . . . again. They are crying. Disobeying you. Talking back to you. Testing your patience. They're just so ungrateful! You want to scream and run away from it all.

But remember, even though they don't seem to appreciate it now, you are giving your children a great gift. Even more, you are giving a gift to God. By caring for your children, you are serving Him for they are His children (as are you). As a parent, you are the Father's earthly surrogate. And He is mighty pleased.

YOUR PROMISE TO GOD . . .

Oh, my Father, I will try to follow Your example and be a caring, loving parent even when my children seem to turn away from me.

PATIENCE

God will reward each of us for what we have done. He will give eternal life to everyone who has patiently done what is good in the hope of receiving glory, honor, and life that lasts forever.

(Romans 2:6–7)

You know that the sacrifices you are making will benefit your family. You know that God is pleased when you are a good steward to His children. So, why is it still so difficult? You don't want to be selfish, but you find yourself wondering what's in it for you. Well, I'll tell you. . . .

Your children are your legacy—a living testament to your godliness. They are your mark on the world. Like the gardener who lovingly tends his crops, your work as a parent will reap fruit for generations to come. And God will reward you . . . in both this life and the one to come. Remain faithful, for God will honor you in more ways than you can know.

Your Promise to God . . .

I will serve You faithfully by serving my family. The work can be hard, but the reward is great.

ANGER

ANGER

A kind answer
   soothes angry feelings,
but harsh words
   stir them up.
      (Proverbs 15:1)

How easy it is to respond to anger with anger. Our children can sometimes bring forth their anger as they learn about boundaries and lessons. We can respond either by getting angry right back at them, or by diffusing the situation by responding with understanding and patience. Now, even as I write these words, I know how hard this is! But it is vital to creating healthy connections with our kids. Turn the anger around! Live in God's patience. God is patient with you, now you can pass that patience on to your children.

YOUR PROMISE TO GOD . . .

Today I will live in Your patience, knowing that every act of anger can be diffused with an act of patience.

ANGER

Don't be angry or furious.
Anger can lead to sin.
(Psalm 37:8)

Many of us learned anger at the hands of our parents and elders. Not anger as a tool to teach when a child does something inappropriate, but anger at their lives, anger at their situations, anger at God. Unknowingly, many of us took that very anger into our own experience. Our parents and elders weren't always equipped to teach us anything other than what they knew, and if anger is what they knew, that is what we learned. The Good News of God is that we can unlearn the anger of our past, and learn the love of our Lord. We can heal from the anger that we've carried for so very long, and instead bestow upon our children the gift of giving joy. Let's not pass along the sins of our elders to the next generation. Become a parent who turns it around.

YOUR PROMISE TO GOD . . .

I turn away from any anger that I inherited and turn it around to the peace of God in my life, and in the life of my family.

ANGER

But I promise you that if you are angry with someone, you will have to stand trial. If you call someone
a fool, you will be taken to court. And if you say
that someone is worthless, you will be in danger of
the fires of hell.

So if you are about to place your gift on the altar and remember that someone is angry with you,
leave your gift there in front of the altar. Make peace
with that person, then come back and offer your gift
to God.

(Matthew 5:22–24)

Jesus tells us something revolutionary: What we do matters. It matters to us, it matters to our children, it matters to the people around us, and it matters to God. We may not know it, but we are not just random lives living a chaotic existence. The plan of God for you, as a parent and as a person, is to rise above the muck and mire of the world and, through the grace of God, be lifted into a new understanding. We are given the charge to respond to anything other than love with love. Not our love, for by ourselves we do not have the ability to do this. Trust me, I've tried! No, not our love but rather with the love of Christ, who can provide you with more love and forgiveness and patience than you can imagine. Make a list right now of everyone who is bugging you, and then begin the journey by offering a prayer about them to God, letting God know you are ready to respond to everything with His love.

YOUR PROMISE TO GOD . . .

The love of God allows me to respond to every situation today with love, His love.

ANGER

My dear friends, you should be quick to listen and slow to speak or to get angry. If you are angry, you cannot do any of the good things that God wants done. You must stop doing anything immoral or evil. Instead be humble and accept the message that is planted in you to save you.

(James 1:19–21)

Isn't it amazing how quick and easy it is to go right to anger in our lives? Parents especially can be provoked to anger so quickly that it can be scary. Our children somehow seem to know exactly which button to push, which nerve to work, to take us immediately to anger. What would God have you do? He would have you know that you have been chosen to be a parent for a reason, that you are uniquely able to be the hands and the heart of the Lord in the life of your children. You are the one that God has called forth to represent Him in your child's life. Does your child feel the love of Christ through you? Today, let God's love shine forth from you right into the heart of your child.

YOUR PROMISE TO GOD . . .

The love of God shines through me today, and I refuse anger and instead choose love.

ANGER

Stop being bitter and angry and mad at others.
Don't yell at one another or curse each other or ever
be rude. Instead, be kind and merciful, and forgive
others, just as God forgave you because of Christ.

(Ephesians 4:31–32)

Children can be loud. Let's get real about this for a second: Children can yell and scream and be dramatic and have fits. Not all the time, but when it happens, watch out! When children get angry, they do not hide it, instead they just let it out. Parents can be loud as well, and let their anger create fits and drama. The difference is this: You are the parent, not the child. You are the example of how to have positive anger, and then take it into a positive resolution. Your job as a parent is to not let your children teach you to be angry, but rather to teach your children how to express themselves positively. That means you must first express yourself positively. You can do it, I know you can!

Your Promise to God . . .

I will be the parent, not the child today. I will express myself positively, and teach my children to do the same.

ANGER

At that time you will say,
"I thank you, Lord!
  You were angry with me,
but you stopped being angry
  and gave me comfort.
I trust you to save me,
Lord God,
  and I won't be afraid.
My power and my strength
come from you,
  and you have saved me."

  (Isaiah 12:1–2)

Sometimes it just gets to be overwhelming. Sometimes being a parent can be exhausting and frustrating. Yes, there are great joys, but at times it is hard to remember the joy for all of the anger that we can feel. At this point, we have one very powerful tool available to us, and that is the power of decision. Decide right now to surrender the anger to God, to surrender the fear behind the anger to God. Decide to ask God to help you to deal with anger in a healthy way, and to help shield your children from any misguided anger. Decide to take a step, no matter how small, to release your anger and embrace God. He will see you through.

Your Promise to God . . .

I decide right now to let go of all anger and resentment and I decide to trust God alone.

HEALING

HEALING

I am the Lord your God.
I am holding your hand,
   so don't be afraid.
I am here to help you.
   (Isaiah 41:13)

Children don't come with an instruction manual. One minute you're pregnant and the next you have a tiny, helpless infant in your arms. That small being is totally dependent on you for everything. What a monumental responsibility! And although you've read books, and perhaps taken classes, you really have no idea what to do or if you're doing it right. Every new parent experiences that fear the first night they have the baby at home. Are they feeding him too much? Not enough? Is she warm enough or bundled too heavily? Is he sleeping too much? Why does he keep on crying? Our natural maternal or paternal instincts are supposed to kick in, but quite frankly we're not too sure of ourselves.

Relax. You really do know exactly what to do. You have a wonderful role model to follow. Our Heavenly Father takes perfect care of His children. He is by your side and will guide you in your exciting new role as parent.

YOUR PROMISE TO GOD . . .

I will not be afraid because You are by my side, guiding me always.

HEALING

*For though your hearts were once full of darkness,
now you are full of light from the Lord, and your
behavior should show it! For this light within you
produces only what is good and right and true.*

Try to find out what is pleasing to the Lord.

(*Ephesians 5:8–10**)

So you haven't always been the model of godliness. You once strayed from the path of righteousness and now you're concerned that you are not worthy to be a parent. Don't you realize that when you handed your sins up to God, He forgave you and washed you clean? Don't you know that He cleared out the darkness from your heart and filled you with Light? Just continue to serve the Lord and you will be a wonderful role model for your children, shining God's bright Light on them and showing them the Way.

YOUR PROMISE TO GOD . . .

I will always try to please You, my Father, and set a good example for my children.

HEALING

Jesus turned around and said to her, "Daughter, be encouraged! Your faith has made you well." And the woman was healed at that moment.

(Matthew 9:22*)

Many parents are suffering from a disease called Supermom or Superdad Syndrome. They try to be and do everything—breadwinner, homework checker, cupcake maker, Little League coach, party planner, carpooler, and the list goes on and on. The problem is: They never ask for help. They try to do it all and then, sooner or later, they burn out, overloaded and overwhelmed by all their duties. And at that point, they're unable to do anything at all. They become exhausted, discouraged, and resentful.

Ask for help! There is Someone who is always there to aid you. Just call out to Him and He will cure your disease. Let God lift you up and get you through. He will never let you down.

YOUR PROMISE TO GOD . . .

I will remember that I can't do it all by myself. But with Your help and guidance I will prevail.

HEALING

Pay attention, my child, to what I say. Listen carefully. Don't lose sight of my words. Let them penetrate deep within your heart, for they bring life and radiant health to anyone who discovers their meaning.

(Proverbs 4:20–22*)

I sometimes think children have a hearing problem. You can talk to them until you're blue in the face, but the words don't seem to penetrate their brains. It's as if your words go in one ear and out the other! But let me tell you, sometimes they're not the only ones suffering from this malady. I know plenty of adults who have the same problem. They go to church, they read their Bible, they even take Bible study classes, but yet they're still walking around griping, worrying, arguing, judging, and committing countless other sins. It seems like the Good Word hasn't penetrated their brains or their hearts. Listen! The Lord has Good News for you, so pay attention! Let His words take root in your heart and love, happiness, and godliness will blossom within you.

YOUR PROMISE TO GOD . . .

I will read the Bible daily and let the Word penetrate my heart.

HEALING

With all my heart
I praise the Lord!
I will never forget
how kind he has been.

The Lord forgives our sins,
heals us when we are sick,
and protects us from death.
His kindness and love
are a crown on our heads.
Each day that we live,
he provides for our needs
and gives us the strength
of a young eagle.

(Psalm 103:2–5)

Being parent can wear you down. You're tired, hurried, harried, and overwhelmed. Sometimes at the end of the day, you just drop into bed, exhausted to the core of your being. Even your bones ache! Before you close your eyes and head into dreamland, take a moment to have a one-on-one with the Lord. Ask Him for help, guidance, and the strength to parent the young charges in your care. He will answer your call and refresh you, raising you up to face another day.

YOUR PROMISE TO GOD . . .

When I think I can't possibly do any more, I will look to You for renewal.

HEALING

Let's do our best
    to know the Lord.
His coming is as certain
    as the morning sun;
he will refresh us like rain
renewing the earth
    in the springtime.
        (Hosea 6:3)

God made a promise to us and Jesus fulfilled it. Through Him we are saved, our sins forgiven. Through Him we have Eternal Life. Through Him we inherit the Kingdom of Heaven. Praise Christ our Lord and serve Him well. Let Him into your home and into your heart. Pray and study Scripture every day and let His Word refresh your soul.

YOUR PROMISE TO GOD . . .

I will endeavor to know You better and joyfully celebrate Your goodness.

GRATITUDE

GRATITUDE

I pray that you will be grateful to God for letting you have part in what he has promised his people in the kingdom of light.

(Colossians 1:12)

Do you know what a powerful tool gratitude can be in your life? If you make a list of everything you are grateful for as a parent, I believe that you will be surprised at how long the list is. Your children are the most precious gifts that God can give, and you get the good pleasure to steward these children. Thank God for His faith in you. It is a mighty privilege that He has bestowed upon you.

YOUR PROMISE TO GOD . . .

Thank You, God. Thank You, God. Thank You, God.

GRATITUDE

The sacrifice that honors me
is a thankful heart.
Obey me, and I, your God,
will show my power to save.
(Psalm 50:23–24)

You do so much for your children, yet they often forget to say "thank you" to you. And you know it as well as I do—your children don't even know the half of what you do on their behalf. Feeling underappreciated can sap you of your joy. Feeling undervalued can create in you a heavy heart, and a resentment toward your family. If I were standing in front of you right now, I would look you in the eye and say to you, "Thank you. Thank you for parenting your children. Thank you for your willingness to grow as a parent. Thank you for every single thing you do for every one of your children. Whether they know it or not, God knows everything you do, and you shall be rewarded."

YOUR PROMISE TO GOD . . .

When I am feeling underappreciated, I will remember that You are grateful for me and everything that I do.

GRATITUDE

You are God's people, so don't let it be said that any of you are immoral or indecent or greedy. Don't use dirty or foolish or filthy words. Instead, say how thankful you are.

(Ephesians 5:3–4)

Miss Marge's daughter is on the honor roll, and neighbor Tyrell's son is a football hero. Sometimes it seems that other people's children shine so brightly. Don't compare your children to anyone else's children, for your children are unique and special in their own ways. They have their own talents, and God will bring those talents forth at the exact right time, in the exact right way—for His glory, not yours. Love your children for who they are, and while you instill in them a good ethic, do not let your love depend on their achievements. God doesn't withhold His love for you. He is grateful for you. Be grateful for your children.

YOUR PROMISE TO GOD . . .

My children are special. I will love them unconditionally.

GRATITUDE

Each one of you is part of the body of Christ, and you were chosen to live together in peace. So let the peace that comes from Christ control your thoughts. And be grateful. Let the message about Christ completely fill your lives, while you use all your wisdom to teach and instruct each other. With thankful hearts, sing psalms, hymns, and spiritual songs to God. Whatever you say or do should be done in the name of the Lord Jesus, as you give thanks to God the Father because of him.

(Colossians 3:15–17)

You cannot be an effective parent, and surround yourself with the low values of the world. How can you expect your children to rise above the world when you are stuck smack-dab in the middle of it? Listen to this advice carefully: Flood your life with positive messages, positive people, and positive thoughts and actions. What we are constantly surrounded by, will directly influence our perceptions and worldview. When you fill your life with gratitude, there will be no room for any of the garbage. Give praise a chance and watch the amazing results.

YOUR PROMISE TO GOD . . .

I will sing Your praises, and fill my home with thanksgiving and positivity.

GRATITUDE

You have accepted Christ Jesus as your Lord. Now keep on following him. Plant your roots in Christ and let him be the foundation for your life. Be strong in your faith, just as you were taught. And be grateful.

(Colossians 2:6–7)

You might measure the worth of your family in terms of dollars, achievements, and trophies on the mantel. I can tell you this for sure: Mistaking your family's success for the rewards of the world is like building a house of cards. One strong wind of adversity and it will all come tumbling down. When you let Jesus be the foundation for your family life, nothing can shake your world. Even in the fiercest storm, the house of the Lord stays firm and strong.

YOUR PROMISE TO GOD . . .

I am grateful that You are my rock, keeping my entire family safe and secure.

GRATITUDE

I thank Christ Jesus our Lord. He has given me the strength for my work because he knew that he could trust me.

(1 Timothy 1:12)

Soccer games, new clothes, parent/teacher conferences, and on and on. It seems like the list of needs from your children is endless. They are constantly needing and wanting more from you. It would be easy to feel taken advantage of, like a well that an entire village uses for their nourishment. But who nourishes you? Where does your strength come from? The answer is easy: from the Lord. God has promised you that He will give you strength, and Jesus even goes as far as to say to give Him your burdens, He will bear them for you. If resentment or feeling at the end of your rope has entered your life, turn it over right now to the Lord. And give Him thanks that even if no one else pats you on the back, God is propping you up.

YOUR PROMISE TO GOD . . .

I promise to remember that You alone fulfill every one of my needs, so that I am able to freely give to my family.

GRATITUDE

You, Lord, are my God!
I will praise you
for doing the wonderful things
you had planned and promised
since ancient times.

(Isaiah 25:1)

As a parent you make a covenant with your child. You promise to care for him, nurture him, teach him, and keep him safe. From even before you received your child, you were planning how to be the best parent you could be, planning all that you could give. It feels good to give to your child, doesn't it? You also made a covenant with the Lord. You promised to faithfully serve Him and care for the little life that He entrusted to you. God has had you in His plan from the start. It was His good pleasure to choose you specifically to parent your children, and it is your good pleasure to thankfully fulfill His plan.

YOUR PROMISE TO GOD . . .

Thank you, God, for choosing me and trusting me to parent my children. I will always aim to serve You and to serve them as best I can.

HARDSHIP

HARDSHIP

Don't follow the bad example
of cruel and evil people.
Turn aside and keep going.
Stay away from them.
(Proverbs 4:14–15)

Your good-time girlfriends were fun when you were single. And now, when you have some hardships, they have plenty of advice to give—none of it positive. But then again, you have grown in the Lord since your time with them. You may have friends that seemed harmless back in the day, but now you wonder if those same friends are really the best influences for your family. What once seemed harmless now seems harmful. The Lord is clear—surround yourself and your loved ones with godly people, people who can help lift you and your children up, not drag you down or bleed you dry. Seek others who live in the Lord, and the Lord will bless your home.

YOUR PROMISE TO GOD . . .

I will be careful about who I let near my children or in my home. I will only invite goodness and godliness into the house.

HARDSHIP

Jesus told his disciples:

Have faith in God! If you have faith in God and don't doubt, you can tell this mountain to get up and jump into the sea, and it will. Everything you ask for in prayer will be yours, if you only have faith.

(Mark 11:22–24)

When things are really looking bleak, remember all you have to do is turn to God. The familiar verse, "ask and you shall receive," is true. I'm not preaching a name-it-and-claim-it sermon here. I'm encouraging you to have a deep-rooted belief that God knows exactly what you need and will always provide for you. Trust in Him even in the darkest moments, and have faith that He will bring you His Light. The more you seek Him, the more He will find you.

Your Promise to God . . .

In my darkest hours, I turn to You. I trust You. I love You. Thank You.

HARDSHIP

And the Scriptures were written to teach and encourage us by giving us hope.

(Romans 15:4)

You might think that life does not come with an instruction manual, but I have Good News for you—it does. It is called the *Bible* and it is filled with tips, rules, and inspirations to guide you on your journey as a parent. Whenever you experience doubt or despair, turn to the Word and let it lift you up. Just as Paul writes in this verse, the *Bible* is the ultimate self-help guide, written by the Creator of all Life. Read it, learn it, live it. By doing so, you will gain practical tools and uplifting motivation for every hardship that comes your way. God doesn't promise to get rid of hardships, but God does promise to help you through each one.

YOUR PROMISE TO GOD . . .

I will read the Bible daily, and look to it for sustenance.

HARDSHIP

God will bless you, if you don't give up when your faith is being tested. He will reward you with a glorious life, just as he rewards everyone who loves him.

(James 1:12)

Sometimes it feels too hard. Sometimes it feels like it would be so much easier to just give it all up. Sometimes being a parent requires too much of your life, or at least, that's how it feels. Where is God when you need Him? Where is God when it seems too hard to bear? Right here, right where you are right this moment God is with you. God is always by your side, hoping that you will turn to Him for help. If you do, you will be given everything you need to make it through whatever you are going through. God's reward is waiting for you. Don't give up! Don't give in! Turn now to God. Reach out to God. He's waiting for you.

YOUR PROMISE TO GOD . . .

I turn to You, dear God, asking for Your help. I will let You guide me for I know You are my beacon.

HARDSHIP

But God shows undeserved kindness to everyone. That's why he appointed Christ Jesus to choose you to share in his eternal glory. You will suffer for a while, but God will make you complete, steady, strong, and firm.

(1 Peter 5:10)

After the day you had at work, the last thing you think you need is whining, complaining, and disobedience from your children. Have you ever had one of those days? Months? Years? Here is a secret that can help: When you see the needs of your children as hardships, it makes everything harder. When you see their needs as opportunities to love, you are actually changing the "hard" into "heart." When you open yourself to your children—especially when you don't feel like you have anything left to give—God can transform your struggle into your blessing.

YOUR PROMISE TO GOD . . .

I give up the struggle and give out the love.

HARDSHIP

I have told you this, so that you might have peace in your hearts because of me. While you are in the world, you will have to suffer. But cheer up! I have defeated the world.

(*John 16:33*)

You are watching the news with your child—how do you explain natural disasters? How do you explain senseless tragedy? How can you explain war and hate and poverty to a child? There are no easy answers. Unfortunately the world is not always a peaceful place. That is why you must have peace in your family, which begins as peace in your own heart. When you feel the safety of the Lord, your children will feel safe as well. Share with your children the promises that God has made. Teach them that God is faithful. When they know this Truth, it won't matter what is on the news because it all has the same solution: God.

YOUR PROMISE TO GOD . . .

I will teach my children to rely on You. You are our Savior.

HAPPINESS

HAPPINESS

Don't worry about anything, but pray about every-thing. With thankful hearts offer up your prayers and requests to God. Then, because you belong to Christ Jesus, God will bless you with peace that no one can completely understand. And this peace will control the way you think and feel.

(Philippians 4:6–7)

You wouldn't knowingly let a thief into your home, inviting him to steal whatever he wanted out of your house, would you? There is no reason why you would do that. And yet, most of us do that very thing every single day—the thief is called "worry." Worry robs us of living in the present moment, it robs us of remembering the gifts that we have in our lives and the abilities God has given us to deal with adversities. Most of all, it robs us of trust and faith in the Living God who is always present, always here to help. It is time— now!—to stop allowing the thief of happiness to enter your life.

YOUR PROMISE TO GOD . . .

I refuse the thief of worry in my life, I embrace happiness in my life.

HAPPINESS

Sing new songs of praise to him;
play skillfully on the harp and sing with joy.

(Psalm 33:3 *)

Have you ever noticed that the things that make us the happiest are the very things that often are the most simple? Many of the happiest memories I have of my family are when we were just together, in the ordinary day-to-day of our lives. Talking, spending time together, laughing, listening, singing, sharing meals—all of those simple things bring joy and happiness to the entire family. Start this week. Set aside time in your lives to just hang out with each other with no agenda other than being together. If you make this a regular habit, it'll have long, positive repercussions in your life, and the lives of everyone in your family.

Your Promise to God . . .

Today the simple joy of loving my family well will bring me happiness.

HAPPINESS

Worry weighs a person down; an encouraging word cheers a person up.

(Proverbs 12:25*)

Here is a parenting tip that seems too simple to be powerful, but remember that most powerful things usually are simple. Every day, say something to your children that is positive. That's it. Every single day, without fail, give your children a compliment, a pat of the back, a high five, a hug, and an "I'm proud of you." When you give your children positive feedback that comes from your heart, it goes directly into their hearts and lives there forever. An encouraging word from you to your child daily will literally help them develop healthy and positive self-attitudes that, in turn, will bless everyone around them. And while you are at it, say something positive to yourself every day. Read the word of God each day to re-center yourself around the Truth of Jesus Christ.

YOUR PROMISE TO GOD . . .

I will give my children positive, heartfelt feedback today, knowing that it will blossom into tomorrow's self-esteem.

HAPPINESS

But for you that honor my name, victory will shine like the sun with healing in its rays, and you will jump around like calves at play.

(Malachi 4:2)

Is God the center of your family? Have you made the Lord the central figure around which your family revolves? By dipping deeply daily into the Word of God, you are literally bringing eternal wisdom into your family. Living from the place of God First, you are setting up a system in the lives of everyone in your family that will develop into a strong way of life for your children as they grow and have families of their own. The priorities you set now for them become the priorities that they carry on into their futures. If you don't already do it, make sure that prayer and daily Bible reading as a family are part of your lives. Even a few minutes reading the Word of God and a short prayer can make a huge difference in your family's experience.

YOUR PROMISE TO GOD . . .

God is first in my life. God is first in my family's life. God is our center.

HAPPINESS

Those who listen to instruction will prosper; those who trust the Lord will be happy.

(Proverbs 16:20*)

There are many families who are poor in happiness, mainly because they don't invest any time or effort into the family. Families, like our relationship with the Lord, benefit from constant depositing of our time and our attention and our love. When we give constantly to our family, we are building up a reserve of love that then can be used by the entire family at any and every time. And the best news is this: The interest that God pays on your deposits are amazing—promises of guidance and love and eternal life. That is an investment worth making for you and for your children.

YOUR PROMISE TO GOD . . .

I invest God's happiness into my family's life, and I know that I and my family will all reap the interest.

HAPPINESS

How I rejoice in God my Savior!
(Luke 1:47*)

The most important lesson we can learn is the lesson of happiness. Where does your happiness come from? From buying expensive things? From keeping up with the neighbors? From trying to make everyone around you happy? Or does your joy come from the Lord, knowing that He loves you right now, right as you are? You see, we often put our joy in the things of this world, the things that are outside of us, the things that do not actually last for more than minutes or hours. You have a choice, however, and that other choice, the better choice, is to draw your joy from the eternal well of God. By knowing that true joy is God, then everything else in your life will have more meaning as well.

YOUR PROMISE TO GOD . . .

I choose God, I choose happiness.

LESSONS

LESSONS

Your laws are my greatest joy!
I follow their advice.

(Psalm 119:24)

Everything that the Bible teaches us is for our own good. Think of it as God loving us through pruning us into all that He would have us be. As parents, we also do that with our children, help them to develop strong actions and attitudes, and help them to overcome fears or unhealthy behaviors. God's lessons can come in many forms, many of them through your children, so, in every situation, ask yourself what God is trying to teach you. Then answer that lesson with the very best that you have inside. Don't forget to ask for God's help!

YOUR PROMISE TO GOD . . .

I delight in God's lessons in my life, and I, in turn, delight in teaching my children.

LESSONS

May God himself, our Father, and our Lord Jesus make it possible for us to come to you very soon. And may the Lord make your love grow and overflow to each other and to everyone else, just as our love overflows toward you. As a result, Christ will make your hearts strong, blameless, and holy when you stand before God our Father on that day when our Lord Jesus comes with all those who belong to him.

(1 Thessalonians 3:11–13*)

There is a freedom in living by the Word of God. This freedom is knowing that the only way out of the prison of our smallness, of our sin, of our past, and of our habits is through the strength and guidance of He who made us. When we learn this Truth, we can begin to live this Truth. And when we live this Truth, it changes the very essence of who we are, which, in turn, changes each person around us. As a parent, you can draw directly on the strength of the Lord in your life—not as a Sunday church service, but right here and right now. Right now, as you are reading these words, let the prayer of surrender come forth; let Jesus into your life and into your family. Make Him an active part of everything you do, and you will be amazed at how strong this will make you, and how quickly your family will respond to it.

YOUR PROMISE TO GOD . . .

I am free in Jesus Christ. I surrender my life to Him.

LESSONS

Obey God's message! Don't fool yourselves by just listening to it. If you hear the message and don't obey it, you are like people who stare at themselves in a mirror and forget what they look like as soon as they leave. But you must never stop looking at the perfect law that sets you free. God will bless you in everything you do, if you listen and obey, and don't just hear and forget.

(James 1:22–25)

Many people go to church, hear the word taught, nod their heads, and then go back to living their lives the way that they have always done. But the Word of God is not something that you just hear and then forget—they are not just nice words in a book that was written long ago. The Word of God is something that can change you from the inside out. It can restructure you to your very soul, and literally make you new again. Parents often get advice from the people around them, from so-called experts on talk shows, from parenting books. But all of the advice in the world won't make any difference in your life if you do not implement it. There is power in taking action. God encourages us to not just hear the Word but to live it. As a parent, that means doing what you can each day for your children, trusting the Lord to do for you what you cannot do.

Your Promise to God . . .

Today I won't just talk about it, I will do it. I will live the higher life that God has in store for me.

LESSONS

"And when you stand praying, if you hold anything against anyone, forgive him, so that your Father in heaven may forgive you your sins."

(Mark 11:25[†])

One of the most important issues for a parent is: forgiveness. Why? You see, forgiveness is a gift that we are given by God, that we can give to others, and that we can give to ourselves. It is our responsibility as parents to forgive those who harmed us before, so that we do not carry and then inflict those same scars onto our children. It is our joy to offer forgiveness to our ourselves for the things that we may have done in the past. And most importantly, seek first the forgiveness of God, so that your life may be made clean again. As we actively make forgiveness a part of our lives, we can offer this forgiveness to our children when they need it. Withholding forgivenss from our children usually comes from a forgiveness we have withheld from someone else. Make forgiving more than a word—make it a priority and a way of life.

Your Promise to God . . .

I freely give forgiveness to my children, knowing I can teach them without withholding love. And I give thanks to God for forgiving me.

LESSONS

Stop being bitter and angry and mad at others.
Don't yell at one another or curse each other or ever
be rude. Instead, be kind and merciful, and forgive
others, just as God forgave you because of Christ.

(Ephesians 4:31–32)

It is amazing how quick parents can be to say something mean or sarcastic to their children, and how slow parents can be to praise or uplift them. God calls us to be tender-hearted, which means to never let the sin of hardness overtake us. This is especially important for parents, because it is so easy to lose sight of the joy of parenting while we are in the midst of the drama of parenting. Returning to your tenderheartedness will allow God to bring joy back into your life, and that will bring joy into your children's lives. If you find yourself saying something cruel or sarcastic or even dispiriting, catch yourself and turn it around. Make the negative become a lesson in becoming positive for you and for your child.

YOUR PROMISE TO GOD . . .

I will think before responding, so that I do not respond with anything other than God's love.

LESSONS

A person without self-control is as defenseless as a city with broken-down walls.

(Proverbs 25:28*)

So many of us hate the word "discipline" but it is essential for a parent to develop the discipline of positive parenting. Learning to have self-control over your emotions and your actions will not only make you a more effective parent, it will also instill the gift of discipline in your children. If life is a journey, most people meander along a little path that has been trampled by the masses. But discipline puts us on a highway toward being the person and the parent that God has called you to be.

Your Promise to God . . .

I live discipline, knowing that freedom comes through discipline. I teach my children healthy discipline, knowing they will benefit from it for a lifetime.

PURPOSE

PURPOSE

So you should not be like cowering, fearful slaves.
You should behave instead like God's very own chil-
dren . . . calling him "Father, dear Father."

(Romans 8:15*)

God is not some distant relative you see only on holidays. He is your Father, and He wants to be part of your life every day. He will give you strength and guidance, love and comfort. With Him in your corner, you can never lose. All He asks in return is that you praise Him. Lift up your voice, open your heart, proclaim His glory. Praise God for everything you have. Praise Him for all that He does. Praise Him for His faithful love and call Him your Father.

YOUR PROMISE TO GOD . . .

God, I praise You for all that You are and all that You do.

PURPOSE

Christ gives me the strength to face anything.
(*Philippians 4:13*)

God has a plan for you. He designed your life and put you exactly where you are today. Don't think you can't walk the path that was set before you. Don't think you aren't strong enough to take on the role He cast you in. When God determined your purpose, He didn't give you something He didn't think you could accomplish. He only gives us that which we can handle. You will face challenges, for only by stretching can we grow, but the Lord will give you the strength you need to succeed.

YOUR PROMISE TO GOD . . .

I want to be the parent You created me to be. I will look to You to show me the way.

PURPOSE

You must accept whatever situation the Lord has put you in, and continue on as you were when God first called you.

(*1 Corinthians 7:17**)

God placed you exactly where He wants you. He has called you to where you are for a reason. He gave you the children you have. He determined that you would be a parent. Oh, how He trusts you! For being a parent is being God's voice and His hands here on Earth. You are charged with tending to young lives, protecting and nurturing God's own children. Let Him use you for His purpose. He will show you the way.

YOUR PROMISE TO GOD . . .

I am here for a reason—to fulfill Your purpose for me. I will walk the path You have laid before me and I will serve You faithfully.

PURPOSE

We know that God is always at work for the good
of everyone who loves him. They are the ones God
has chosen for his purpose,

(Romans 8:28)

Let me tell you something you may not know, but secretly have hoped for all of your life: God has chosen you for a special purpose. As a parent, your purpose is to love and grow your children into healthy adults, who have God as their Source and love as their aim. That great purpose was so special that God chose YOU for this mission. Accept the mission in the spirit in which it was given to you—a great compliment from God, who knows you are up for the challenge.

YOUR PROMISE TO GOD . . .

Lord, I am ready, willing, and able to take on this mission that You have set before me.

PURPOSE

The apostles often met together and prayed with a single purpose in mind. The women and Mary the mother of Jesus would meet with them, and so would his brothers.

(Acts 1:14)

Prayer is essential in the life of a parent. Pray for strength to be the best parent you can be. Pray for guidance and help each step of the way. Pray that Jesus will inspire you. Pray for the protection of your family, and for every need being met. Pray for your children, that they may hear Him in your every word. Pray for the patience of Job, and the wisdom of Solomon. Pray for yourself, that you receive the gift of your children freely and fully. Pray for God to always be at the center of your parenting, so that you are led by Him each and every day. Prayer is the first thing to do in every situation, not the last resort!

YOUR PROMISE TO GOD . . .

I will pray to You for guidance and strength. I know You always answer our prayers.

PURPOSE

He will lead children and parents to love each other more, so that when I come, I won't bring doom to the land.

(Malachi 4:6)

God actually requires you to learn the lessons of love in your role as a parent. He specifically asks you to turn to love rather than anger or past hurts when dealing with your children. When your child upsets you, love him through it. When your child gets in trouble, love him through it. When your child needs a hug or cries at night, love him through it. When your child speaks harshly or makes a wrong choice, love him through it. Your love is the most powerful tool you have in raising your children. As God loves you, so should you love your children. That kind of love isn't sugary and too sweet—that kind of love is fierce and protective and corrective. It's loving your children enough to see the best in them, and then expect it from them.

YOUR PROMISE TO GOD . . .

I will love my child and I will love You. It is through love that we remain strong.

FULFILLMENT

FULFILLMENT

"We tell you the good news: What God promised our fathers he has fulfilled for us, their children, by raising up Jesus. As it is written in the second Psalm:

" 'You are my Son;
today I have become your Father.' "

(Acts 13:32–33†)

Do you put the Lord at the center of your family? Over and over God makes it clear that He wants to be the one and only center around which your family life revolves. It is your sacred duty to God to instill the love and knowledge of Jesus into the little lives of your children. Each child has their own path to follow, but a firm foundation in the Lord will give them an internal compass to keep them on firm ground

YOUR PROMISE TO GOD . . .

I will put You at the center of my family and instill in my children a deep love for You.

FULFILLMENT

When morning comes,
let your love satisfy
*   all our needs.*
Then we can celebrate
and be glad for what time
*   we have left.*

(Psalm 90:14)

It's a cliché, I know, but that doesn't mean it isn't true. Cherish every moment you can with your children, because before you know it they are grown up and out of the house. And cherishing every moment does something else— it lets your children know they are cherished by you, just as you are cherished by God the Father. Let today be a day of cherishing and joy. When you do that, you will end the day feeling as if you had truly lived it, rather than just barely making it through. Your children are watching, and they will cherish you as well.

YOUR PROMISE TO GOD . . .

I will cherish my family, and I will cherish You, my Lord.

FULFILLMENT

*Carry each other's burdens, and in this way you
will fulfill the law of Christ.*

(Galatians 6:2†)

Christ carried our burdens right to the cross. He asks only that we accept and follow Him in our lives. By doing this, we learn to be more like Him in our own lives. Don't do it alone. Don't turn your back on letting others help you. Being a parent is hard work, and God has sent you help in the form of family and friends who want to help. Don't let pride stand in the way of what can be a great service to you and your children. In this way, you are letting the Lord care for you, through the arms and hearts and hands of those who love you most. Your children will see these great acts of love, and grow up naturally emulating them. What a great gift—praise God!

Your Promise to God . . .

Dear Jesus, I will let You take care of me, for I cannot do anything without You.

FULFILLMENT

The Lord promised to do many good things for Israel, and he kept his promise every time.

(Joshua 21:45)

Our God is a faithful God, and His promises are not made in vain. Do not think that you are a parent by accident, or that you are not up to the challenge of parenthood. God has chosen you specifically to take care of the beautiful children He has placed in your life. He will help you each step of the way. Ask Him for help. Open your heart to Him, and allow Him to bless you. True fulfillment as a parent can only come from relying on God the Father to lead and guide you.

YOUR PROMISE TO GOD . . .

God, You have given me the gift of parenthood and I thank You mightily for the honor.

FULFILLMENT

You will pray to him, and he will hear you, and you will fulfill your vows to him.

(Job 22:27*)

Sometimes a parent can feel alone, lonely, and even depressed. There are stories every day in the newspapers of parents who didn't get help when they needed it. God never intended you to feel alone, because He is always with you. The Lord is your strength, your protector, and your friend. He is waiting for you to turn to Him—fully and completely—and He will bring you comfort and joy. Isn't it great to know that we are never alone?

YOUR PROMISE TO GOD . . .

When I feel lonely and depressed, I will turn to You, my Lord, and I will never be alone.

FULFILLMENT

Then I will always sing praises to your name
as I fulfill my vows day after day.
(*Psalm 61:8**)

Children feel fulfilled when parents keep their promises. When your child came into your life, you made a vow with God that you would look after this child, not just for days or months or years, but for your whole life. Take that vow seriously. Commit yourself fully to the raising of your children. Being a parent who fulfills every promise you make to your children creates children who feel fulfilled and happy.

YOUR PROMISE TO GOD . . .

You have entrusted me with a great responsibility, and I will commit myself to fulfilling the role You have set before me.

PROMISE
PAGES

PROMISES FROM GOD

Lord, it is tough being a parent, but I know that You have promised me . . .

_____

_____

_____

_____

_____

_____

_____

_____

_____

_____

_____

_____

_____

_____

_____

and You always fulfill Your promises!

PROMISES TO GOD

You give me everything I need to be a good parent, and only ask in return that I am faithful to You. Lord, I promise You I will . . .

and I will strive to be Your faithful servant.

PROMISES FROM GOD

Lord, it is tough being a parent, but I know that You have promised me . . .

_____

_____

_____

_____

_____

_____

_____

_____

_____

_____

_____

_____

_____

_____

_____

_____

_____

and You always fulfill Your promises!

PROMISES TO GOD

You give me everything I need to be a good parent, and only ask in return that I am faithful to You. Lord, I promise You I will . . .

and I will strive to be Your faithful servant.

PROMISES FROM GOD

Lord, it is tough being a parent, but I know that You have promised me . . .

_____

_____

_____

_____

_____

_____

_____

_____

_____

_____

_____

_____

_____

_____

_____

and You always fulfill Your promises!

PROMISES TO GOD

You give me everything I need to be a good parent, and only ask in return that I am faithful to You. Lord, I promise You I will . . .

and I will strive to be Your faithful servant.

PROMISES FROM GOD

Lord, it is tough being a parent, but I know that You have promised me . . .

_____

_____

_____

_____

_____

_____

_____

_____

_____

_____

_____

_____

_____

_____

_____

and You always fulfill Your promises!

PROMISES TO GOD

You give me everything I need to be a good parent, and only ask in return that I am faithful to You. Lord, I promise You I will . . .

and I will strive to be Your faithful servant.

PROMISES FROM GOD

Lord, it is tough being a parent, but I know that You have promised me . . .

_____

_____
_____
_____
_____
_____
_____
_____
_____
_____
_____
_____
_____
_____
_____
_____
_____

and You always fulfill Your promises!

PROMISES TO GOD

You give me everything I need to be a good parent, and only ask in return that I am faithful to You. Lord, I promise You I will . . .

_____

_____

_____

_____

_____

_____

_____

_____

_____

_____

_____

_____

_____

_____

_____

and I will strive to be Your faithful servant.

PROMISES FROM GOD

Lord, it is tough being a parent, but I know that You have promised me . . .

_____

_____

_____

_____

_____

_____

_____

_____

_____

_____

_____

_____

_____

_____

_____

_____

and You always fulfill Your promises!

PROMISES TO GOD

You give me everything I need to be a good parent, and only ask in return that I am faithful to You. Lord, I promise You I will . . .

and I will strive to be Your faithful servant.

PROMISES FROM GOD

Lord, it is tough being a parent, but I know that You have promised me . . .

and You always fulfill Your promises!

PROMISES TO GOD

You give me everything I need to be a good parent, and only ask in return that I am faithful to You. Lord, I promise You I will . . .

_____

_____

_____

_____

_____

_____

_____

_____

_____

_____

_____

_____

_____

_____

_____

and I will strive to be Your faithful servant.

PROMISES FROM GOD

Lord, it is tough being a parent, but I know that You have promised me . . .

_____

_____

_____

_____

_____

_____

_____

_____

_____

_____

_____

_____

_____

_____

and You always fulfill Your promises!

PROMISES TO GOD

You give me everything I need to be a good parent, and only ask in return that I am faithful to You. Lord, I promise You I will . . .

_____

_____

_____

_____

_____

_____

_____

_____

_____

_____

_____

_____

_____

_____

_____

and I will strive to be Your faithful servant.

PROMISES FROM GOD

Lord, it is tough being a parent, but I know that You have promised me . . .

_____

_____

_____

_____

_____

_____

_____

_____

_____

_____

_____

_____

_____

_____

_____

and You always fulfill Your promises!

PROMISES TO GOD

You give me everything I need to be a good parent, and only ask in return that I am faithful to You. Lord, I promise You I will . . .

and I will strive to be Your faithful servant.

PROMISES FROM GOD

Lord, it is tough being a parent, but I know that You have promised me . . .

and You always fulfill Your promises!

PROMISES TO GOD

You give me everything I need to be a good parent, and only ask in return that I am faithful to You. Lord, I promise You I will . . .

and I will strive to be Your faithful servant.

PROMISES FROM GOD

Lord, it is tough being a parent, but I know that You have promised me . . .

_____

_____

_____

_____

_____

_____

_____

_____

_____

_____

_____

_____

_____

_____

and You always fulfill Your promises!

PROMISES TO GOD

You give me everything I need to be a good parent, and only ask in return that I am faithful to You. Lord, I promise You I will . . .

and I will strive to be Your faithful servant.